LIFE OF A COMPLEX MAN

WLR JR.

Paperback: 978-1-969919-59-6
eBook: 978-1-969919-60-2
Library of Congress Control Number: 2025923240

This is a work of fiction.

Ordering Information:

Seven Chapter Literary
201 Helen Walton Drive Suite #2
Tomah WI 54660

Printed in the United States of America

Introduction

In the quiet moments between dawn
and day, when the world is bathed in a
gentle, ethereal light, there lies a space
where the soul finds its true expression.
This is the realm where the poetry of Will
Roberts Jr. breathes, transcending the
ordinary and touching the sacred.
This book of Poetry is not merely a
collection of verses; it is an invitation
to embark on a spiritual journey,
to explore the depths of the human spirit and
the divine whispers that guide our existence.

Each poem in this collection serves as a
beacon, illuminating the path toward inner
peace and understanding. With every line,
Robert's weaves a tapestry of introspection
and revelation, drawing readers into a
world where the mundane transforms into
the miraculous. His words resonate with
the timeless wisdom of the ages, echoing
the universal truths that bind us all.

Roberts' poetry is a testament to the power of the written word to heal, inspire, and awaken the spirit. It calls upon us to pause, reflect, and reconnect with the essence of who we are. In these pages, you will find solace in times of sorrow, joy in moments of despair, and a profound sense of connection to the greater whole.

As you delve into Robert's Poetry allow yourself to be open to the experience. Let the rhythm of the verses and the beauty of the imagery guide you to a place of stillness and serenity. Embrace the journey, and discover the spiritual richness that lies within each poem, waiting to be uncovered.

Welcome to "Life Of A Complex Man, A Collection Of Poetry" by Will Roberts Jr.—a sanctuary for the soul and a celebration of the sacred in everyday life.

Christopher D. Collier
Senior Past or Victorious Life Church
Kansas City, Mo.

The Life of a Complex Man

IT ALL SEEMED SO WONDERFUL
MANY YEARS AGO.
NO WORRIES, NO TROUBLES,
NO RESPONSIBILITIES.

FREE TO DREAM AND LOOK
FORWARD TO THE FUTURE.
EACH DAY WAS FRESH AND
ALIVE WITH NEWNESS.

I WOULD HAVE NEVER IMAGINED
THIS WOULD BE MY STATE.
MAYBE I WAS NAIVE AND REALLY
COULDN'T SEE REALITY.

BECAUSE REALITY TENDS TO
BE A BIT MORE HARSH.
I WAS INEXPERIENCED AND
NOT NEARLY AS ABUSED.

BACK THEN I WAS ALLOWED TO
BE A LOT MORE SELFISH.
INDEED THE WORLD WAS TRULY MINE.

BUT NOW I LOOK BACK AND SEE
IT WAS NEVER REALLY SO.
HINDSIGHT IS TWENTY/TWENTY
ALWAYS MUCH CLEARER.

YES, THE DAYS ALL SEEM THE SAME
EVEN THE YEARS SEEM UNCHANGED.
DEJA VU SEEMS TO HAPPEN
MUCH TOO OFTEN.

IT'S MUCH EASIER NOW TO EXPECT
THINGS WITH HUMBLENESS
GREAT EXPECTATIONS HAVE BEEN
EXPOSED TO BE NOT SO GREAT.

EXPERIENCE MAY BE THE BEST TEACHER
BUT ITS METHOD IS NOT KINDNESS.
HEARTACHE IS INEVITABLE YET I BELIEVE
I'LL STILL GO FORWARD.

THE FUTURE SEEMS HOPEFUL YET
NOTHING UNEXPECTANT.
LIFE TRULY IS A STRUGGLE ONLY
THE STRONG SURVIVE.

I'VE COME TO A CROSSROAD AND
I MUST DECIDE QUICKLY.
FOR I'M SINKING IN DESPAIR AND
MY FEET FEEL LIKE LEAD.

MY PHYSICAL STRENGTH
SURRENDERED LONG, LONG, AGO.
I'M WISE ENOUGH TO KNOW TRUE
STRENGTH IS IN THE MIND.

I WILL SUMMON THE RESOURCES
WITHIN MY SPIRIT.
FOR I CANNOT TRUST IN MY SENSES.
I WILL USE MY PAST FOR MY FUTURE.

YES, I WILL BE GRAY AND WISE.
I'VE LOVED HARD, MAYBE TOO HARD.
YET I'M STRONGER FOR IT, I'M
ALL THE MORE WISE.

YOU KNOW THIS WISDOM THING IS
SIMPLE YET IT'S SO COMPLEX.
I FEEL MYSELF MOVING AGAIN
AND I UNDERSTAND WHY.

THE ROAD I CHOOSE IS THE ROAD I CHOSE.
ONCE AGAIN I MAKE MY CHOICE.
CAREFUL NOW, MANY DANGERS AHEAD.
I KNOW NOW IT DOESN'T MAKE
TOO MUCH DIFFERENCE.

AS I MOVE FORWARD ONCE
AGAIN STEP BY STEP,
I LOOK BACK MANY YEARS AT
MANY DIFFERENT CHOICES.
I QUIETLY SAY TO MYSELF AS I TURN
AND MOVE FORWARD.....................
WOULDN'T CHANGE A THING.

A Test of Faith

MY SPIRIT IS WILLING, BUT
MY FLESH IS KILLING.
MY STEDFAST WALK, MY ENCOURAGING TALK.

FEELING A SENSE OF LETTING GOD DOWN,
NO LONGER STANDING ON SOLID GROUND.

UNSURE OF EVERY STEP,
ALWAYS LOOKING BACK.
OLD LUST I'VE KEPT, SATAN
KNOWS WHERE I LACK.

INSTABILITY IN GOD'S SECURITY,
WHY FACE THAT AS A REALITY.

I KNOW I'M A CHILD OF GOD
AND ALWAYS WILL BE,
BUT MY LACK OF CONTROL IS KILLING ME.

TO GOD BE THE GLORY, FLESH
YOU HAVE LOST.
SALVATION'S STORY, THE LIFE OF
CHRIST IS WHAT IT COST

BUT HE DID THAT FREELY HIS LOVE FOR ME,
MY SPIRIT IN BONDAGE IS NOW SET FREE.

SO IN THE NAME OF JESUS
SATAN FLEE FROM ME,
FOR I AM DESTINED TO BE, WITH
CHRIST, ETERNALLY.

Lord, How Long

LORD, HOW LONG SHALL YOU
DELAY YOUR COMING?
BECAUSE MY SOUL GROWS WEARY
BUT I'LL KEEP ON RUNNING.

LORD, HOW LONG WILL I BE IN THIS FLESH?
BECAUSE MY SPIRIT GROWS
IMPATIENT AS TIME GROWS LESS.

LORD, HOW LONG WILL I SEE SUCH SIN?
BECAUSE THIS IS NOT NATURAL
FOR ME TO BE IN.

LORD, HOW LONG BEFORE
YOU DEAL WITH SA TAN?
BECAUSE IT'S HIS ORIGINAL SIN
AGAINST YOU I'M HATING.

LORD, HOW LONG SHALL MY
KNOWLEDGE BE SMALL?
BECAUSE YOUR PURE KNOWLEDGE
HELPS ME STAND AND NOT FALL.

LORD, HOW LONG DOES IT
TAKE TO BE TRULY PURE?
BECAUSE LORD WHATEVER IT TAKES
I'M WILLING TO ENDURE.

LORD, HOW LONG IS ETERNITY WITH YOU?
BECAUSE WITH YOU THERE'S
SO MUCH I WANT TO DO.

LORD, HOW LONG WILL IT TAKE
FOR ME TO BE LIKE YOU?
BECAUSE IT'S TRUE,
IT'S YOU THAT I WANT THROUGH
AND THROUGH.

LORD, HOW LONG WILL I BE
A WRETCH UNDONE?
BECAUSE I LONG TO HEAR YOU SAY
FAITHFUL SERVANT, WELL DONE.

LORD, HOW LONG WILL QUESTIONS
LIKE THESE BE IN MY MIND?
BECAUSE I KNOW ONCE I'M LIKE YOU,
ANSWERS TO ALL THESE
QUESTIONS I WILL FIND.

LORD, HOW LONG, LORD HOW
LONG, HOW LONG?
THIS QUESTION WITHIN ME IS TRULY STRONG,
BECAUSE LORD TO THEE I BELONG.

No Ordinary Mother

WHAT IS THE DEFINITION OF A MOTH ER.......
IT'S TRUE, EVERYONE HAS THEIR OWN
DEFINITION OF WHAT A MOTHER IS.

I WILL ATTEMPT TO EXPRESS MY IDEAS,
MY THOUGHTS ON WHAT MY MOTHER IS.
THOUGH WORDS, IN MY OPINION
CANNOT TRULY EXPRESS THE
DEPTHS OF WHAT I TRULY FEEL.

YOU ARE MORE THAN ONE COULD
WISH FOR OR DREAM OF
MORE THAN MOST COULD IMAGINE.
THE LIKELIHOOD OR CHANCES
OF YOU WOULD BE
WHAT THEY CALL, ONCE IN A LIFETIME.

HOW FORTUNATE AM I TO CALL YOU MOTHER,
HOW BLESSED AM I TO HAVE YOUR LOVE.
THE TOTALITY OF YOU SEEMS
FROM AN UNEXPLAINABLE FORCE,
AN UNEXPLAINABLE LOVE.

I STRUGGLE WITH THE ABILITY YOU
POSSESS TO BE YOU, TO BE MY MOTHER.
YOU ARE NOT PERFECT BUT A PERFECTION
OF LOVE RESIDES WITHIN YOU AND
PENETRATES MY HEART SO EFFORTLESSLY

GOD IS LOVE, THIS IS TRUE, MY
MOTHER IS LOVE, THIS ALSO IS A
TRUE STATEMENT OF TRUTH.
MY MOTHER IS NO ORDINARY MOTHER
BECAUSE SHE POSSESS NO ORDINARY LOVE.

I WAS BIRTHED IN LOVE BY A WOMAN
OF LOVE, NO ORDINARY THING BUT
INDEED A SPECIAL MIRACLE.
THE WORDS ESCAPE ME BUT MY
INTENTIONS ARE TO TELL YOU WHAT
YOU HAVE BIRTHED PHYSICALLY,
EMOTIONALLY AND SPIRITUALLY IN ME IS
INDEED NOT ORDINARY, BUT ETERNAL.

TO MY MOTHER:
MATTIE GRACE ROBERTS SR

Love Covers

LOVE COVERS THE PAIN WE
CREATE FOR OURSELVES/
LOVE COVERS THE ATTITUDE THAT REBELS.

LOVE COVERS THE ACT OF
ONLY SEEING SELF/
LOVE COVERS OUR DESIRES
AND GREED FOR WEALTH.

LOVE COVERS THE LURE AND
ATTRACTION OF OUR LUST/
LOVE COVERS THE HEART
THAT HAS NO TRUST.

LOVE COVERS OUR DOUBTS
AND ALSO OUR FEARS/
LOVE COVERS ALL OUR SORROWS
DISPLAYED BY MANY TEARS.

LOVE COVERS OUR EMOTIONS THOSE
MISPLACED AND CONFUSED/
LOVE COVERS THE MIND THROUGH ITS PAST
THAT HAS BEEN ABUSED.

LOVE COVERS THE LIE THAT
CUT TO THE HEART/
LOVE COVERS OUR DISAPPOINTMENTS
AND OUR REJECTIONS BEFORE THEY START.

LOVE COVERS OUR GRIEF FROM
LIFE ON THROUGH DEATH/
LOVE COVERS OUR DEEDS FROM
THE RIGHT HAND TO THE LEFT.

LOVE COVERS OUR SOUL, CONNECTING
US, FORMING A BINDING TIE/
LOVE COVERS IT ALL AND THIS
MY FRIEND IS WHY.

ONE DAY LOVE COVERED A WOODEN CROSS,
IT BLED AND IT DIED/
BUT LOVE ROSE IN VICTORY,
FOR US THIS GREAT LOVE WAS APPLIED.

SO WILL WE LIVE FOR OURSELVES
AND ALLOW SIN TO ABIDE/
GOD FORBID THAT LOVE,
THIS THE GREATEST OF LOVE
SHOULD BE DENIED.

Someday We'll Be Free

WHAT WE ALL WANT IS PEACE THROUGHOUT
THE LAND BUT TELL ME WHY DO YOU
SEE SIN WHICH CORRUPTS ALL MAN

TAKE YOU FOR A TRIP BACK IN TIME
WHEN A MAN TOOK HIS LIPS TO
THE FRUIT OF ALL CRIME.

EYES NOW OPEN TO SEE THE MASTER
OF SIN SO NOW THE DOOR WAS MADE
OPEN FOR HIM TO ENTER IN.

THE KNOWLEDGE OF RIGHT AND
WRONG BECAME REALITY SO NOW WE
WONDER WHEN WILL WE BE FREE.

I THINK THE QUESTION SHOULD BE
HOW SHOULD WE BE FREE FROM
THE GRIP OF SIN FOR ETERNITY.

MANY PEOPLE INSIST ON LIVING A LIFE
SO COLD NEVER TAKING CONCERN
FOR THE CARE OF THEIR SOUL.

BUT THE SOUL IS EVERLASTING IT
SHALL LIVE AND HAVE NO PASSING.

THE MASTER OF SIN HAS A FATE TO
FACE HE'S TAKING MANY SERVANTS
WITH HIM TO THIS PLACE.

MAN CREATED A DILEMMA FOR HIMSELF
NOW HE'S GOT A CHOICE TO MAKE
FOR HIS OWN COMMONWEALTH.

THERE'S A CHOICE TO BE MADE AND YOU
CAN'T DENY THAT YOU NEVER MADE YOUR
CHOICE WHEN YOU FACE HIM ON HIGH.

YES, LIFE'S A BATTLE BUT THE WAR HAS
BEEN WON GIVING GLORY TO GOD
THROUGH JESUS CHRIST THE SON.

SO, LIVE A LIFE OF VICTORY NOT A LIFE OF
DEFEAT, AND KNOW YOUR NAME IS IN THAT
NUMBER AND THAT YOU DO HAVE A SEAT.

IN HEAVENLY PLACES WITH HIM WHOSE
LIGHT IS BRIGHT AND NOT DIM.

HE GAVE YOU KNOWLEDGE OF THE KEY
THAT SOMEDAY WE WILL BE FREE.

Lion of Judah

COME LET US REASON TOGETHER FOR
I HAVE MUCH TO TELL,
YOU'VE COME A LONG WAY NOW
PLEASE LISTEN WELL.

FOR THE WISDOM I SHARE
SHALL HELP YOU EXCEL,
NEW LEVELS OF MATURITY ARE
WHERE YOU SHALL DWELL.

BE STILL AND LET MY PEACE PREVAIL,
I ALONE HAVE WHAT YOUR SOUL
DESIRES TO ALLOW ME TO UNVEIL.

TRUE LIFE IS A MYSTERY BUT MY
WORDS SHALL FORETELL, ALL IS
WITHIN ME I URGE YOU TO IMPEL.

COME CLOSER MUCH CLOSER
REMEMBER I RENT THE VEIL, STEP INTO
FAITH INDEED NOW IT PREVAILS.

ALLOW ME TO GIVE YOU PURPOSE AND JOY
ON A WHOLE NEW SCALE.
ONLY BELIEVE IN ME AND YOU CANNOT FAIL.

BY NOW YOU SEE MUCH CLEARER
YOUR SOUL CRIES IT IS WELL.
YOU'VE COME TO ACCEPT MY PERSONA
MY NATURE NOW INDWELLS.

NOW WE ARE ONE WE CAN SHARE
THE MOST INTIMATE DETAILS,
YOU HAVE COME TO KNOW
WHY MY LOVE AVAILS.

INDEED, YOU ARE HOME YOU'VE
REACHED THE END OF YOUR TRIAL,
NOW YOU SEE AND YOU CRY,
"LION OF JUDAH WHO REIGNS
ALL HAIL, ALL HAIL."

Deep Responding To Deep

WHAT I WRITE IS MEANT TO
REACH THE INSIDE,
DEEP CALLING UNTO DEEP.
SO, IF YOU UNDERSTAND ME,
IT'S GODLY UNDERSTANDING.
ALLOW ME TO SHARE MY GOD.

LIFE AS WE KNOW IT IS WHAT?
DEFINE LIFE AND DEFINE ONESELF.
IS IT A SEARCH? INDEED, IT IS.
NOW SEARCH MY WORDS,
SEARCH MY INSIDES.

PASS FROM PHYSICAL TO
SPIRITUAL AND COME CLOSE.
THE FEAR OF THE LORD IS THE
BEGINNING OF WISDOM.
WISDOM BEGINS WITH LISTENING,
LISTENING BEGINS WITH HUMBLENESS,
AND HUMBLENESS BEGINS WITH GOD.

NOW YOU SEE YET MUCH
MORE IS REACHABLE.
COME CLOSER YET, FEEL MY
GOD'S PRESENCE.
FORGETTING ALL BUT HIM,
NOW WHAT DO YOU SEE?
YOU SEE ETERNITY FROM
WHENCE YOU COME.

BIGGER THAN YOURSELF, YET
YOU UNDERSTAND.
THE LOWER THE HIGHER, THE
HIGHER THE LOWER.
FOR THIS IS GOD'S WAY AND
IT'S BEYOND MAN.
IT'S HEAVEN, IT'S HIS ESSENCE, FOR IT IS HIM.

COME CLOSER YET, AND
REMEMBER GOD IS TERRIBLE.
HIS WRATH IS LOVING-KINDNESS.
HIS PERSONA IS A FIRE WHICH BURNS TRUTH.
COME CLOSER AND BE BURNED
TO A CLEANSING.

COME CLOSER YET, FOR YOU
MUST BECOME COMPLETE.
HOME BEYOND HOME, ONE BEYOND ONE.
THIS IS WHERE YOU BELONG,
IT'S YOUR DESTINY.
FIGHTING ONLY BRINGS SELF
CLOSER TO SELF.

YOU BELONG TO HIM, YOU MUST
CONFORM TO YOUR GOD.
BE NOT LOST, BUT FIND YOUR INNER PEACE,
YOUR TRUE MEANING.

DEEP CALLS UNTO DEEP,
YOU HEAR HIM BECAUSE IT'S WHO YOU ARE.
DENYING HIM MEANS DENYING
YOURSELF, HEAR HIM.

I need Your Help

SUPPLY WHAT IS NEEDED, WHO,
OR WHAT CAN DO THAT.
HOW OFTEN DO WE FIND
OURSELVES IN THIS POSITION?

DO WE EVER GET AN ANSWER,
ARE WE EVER SATISFIED?
KNOWING GOD SEEMS TO BE
THE ANSWER YET EVEN THEN WE
FIND OURSELVES WANTING.

LIFE IS EVER-CHANGING, FOREVER
CHALLENGING OUR FAITH.
I'M SEARCHING WITHIN MYSELF
FOR AN ANSWER, FOR A RELIEF.

THINGS SEEM REDUNDANT, I SEARCHED
FOR THE SIMPLICITY TO IT ALL.
YET THE ONLY WAY OF ESCAPE SEEMS
TO BE WORDS THEN MORE WORDS.

TIME IS TAKING ONE DAY AT A TIME.
SURELY THINGS WILL WORK
THEMSELVES OUT IS MY BELIEF.

THAT'S ALL THAT GIVES ME COMFORT,
THE PRESENT SEEMS FAR TOO DEPRESSING.
YET I EXIST NOW AND THAT IS
UNESCAPABLE, UNSHAKABLE.

HERE LIES THE PROBLEM WHO OR
WHAT CAN SUPPLY MY NEED.

IS IT YOU? FOR YOU CAN ONLY OFFER
YOUR OPINIONS OR YOUR BELIEF.
I WANT THE TRUTH THERE ARE
NO ANSWERS IN OPINIONS.

SO THEN WE COME TO THE TRUTH,
WHICH IS STILL HEAVILY DEBATED.
SO YOU READ THIS YET YOU
TRULY CAN'T HELP ME.

BUT WILL YOU TRY? BECAUSE YOU
FEEL YOU HAVE THE TRUTH.
OR WILL YOU DISMISS ME BECAUSE
YOU'RE SEARCHING LIKE ME.

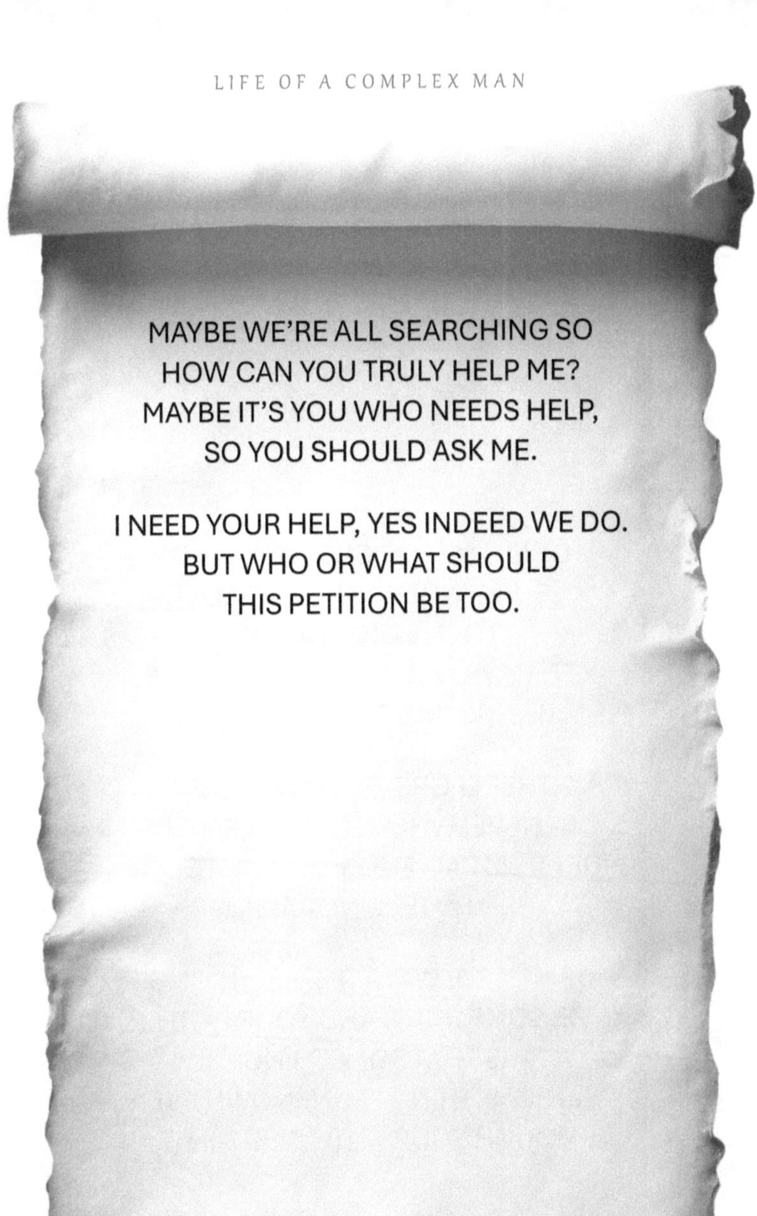
MAYBE WE'RE ALL SEARCHING SO
HOW CAN YOU TRULY HELP ME?
MAYBE IT'S YOU WHO NEEDS HELP,
SO YOU SHOULD ASK ME.

I NEED YOUR HELP, YES INDEED WE DO.
BUT WHO OR WHAT SHOULD
THIS PETITION BE TOO.

Knowledge Beyond Death

DEATH MEANS GIVING UP AND
SURRENDERING YOURSELF
TO THE UNKNOWN.
YET, YOUR FAITH LIVES ON, YOU'LL
REST IN WHAT YOU BELIEVE.

THEREFORE, WHAT DO YOU
BELIEVE, WHERE IS YOUR FAITH
DEATH IS PAINFULLY UNDERSTOOD
WHEN FAITH IS NOT APPLIED.

DEATH IS ALWAYS THE BEGINNING
OF SOMETHING AND YOUR FAITH
IS THAT SOMETHING.
THIS SOMETHING IS UNKNOWN EVEN
THOUGH YOUR FAITH RESTS IN IT.

MANY PEOPLE FEAR THE UNKNOWN;
THEREFORE, THEY FEAR DEATH.
DEATH THEN IS NOT FEARED,
IT'S WHAT'S ON THE OTHER SIDE
OF DEATH THAT PEOPLE FEAR.

ESTABLISH THE UNKNOWN THEN THE
UNKNOWN CANNOT BE FEARED.
THERE IS NO FEAR IN FAITH, FAITH
LIVES IN THE UNKNOWN, WHICH
IS THE OTHER SIDE OF DEATH.

WE NOW CAN SEE THAT WHAT
WE BELIEVE OR HAVE FAITH IN IS
ESTABLISHED DURING THIS LIFE.
UNDERSTAND THAT THIS LIFE IS TO
ESTABLISH OUR FAITH IN THE UNKNOWN.

TRULY THE QUESTION OF
WHERE IS YOUR FAITH IS
APPROPRIATE FOR US ALL.
OUR FAITH SOLIDIFIES OUR FUTURE
WITHIN THE UNKNOWN.

OH DEATH WHERE IS THY STING,
WHERE IS YOUR VICTORY?
I AM A CREATION CREATED BY
FAITH WHOSE FULL OF FAITH.

I REST NOW KNOWING SOMEWHERE
BEYOND TIME I WILL AWAKEN.
ONLY TO BEHOLD THAT FROM
WHENCE I'VE ORIGINATED AND THAT
WHICH I'VE ALWAYS KNOWN.

Jesus Loves Me

JESUS LOVES ME THIS I KNOW,
FOR THE BIBLE TELLS ME SO.

AND HOW DID HE EXPRESS HIS LOVE FOR
ME, HE DIED ON THE CROSS AND SUFFERED
TO THE HIGHEST DEGREE.

BUT WHEN HE ROSE AGAIN HE'D
CONQUERED ALL SIN,
TO PROVE HE WAS GOD AS
HE ALWAYS HAD BEEN.

WE MUST HOLD STRONG TO OUR
FAITH AND LIVE AS HE,
YOU ARE NOT ALONE, HIS HOLY
SPIRIT DWELLS WITHIN THEE.

WE ARE ONLY HUMAN, SOMETIMES
WE MAY GO WRONG,
REMEMBER AGAIN YOU'VE
GOT JESUS HE WON'T LEAVE YOU ALL ALONE.

WE'LL LIVE A VICTORIOUS LIFE
WITH CONTINUAL ATONEMENT
FOR OUR SINS, BUT IT SHALL ALL
BE DONE WHEN OUR SAVIOUR
GOD RETURNS TO US AGAIN.

Could this be Hell

COULD THIS BE HELL.....
CUZ WHERE ELSE COULD
YOU FIND SUCH EVIL

COULD THIS BE HELL.....
CUZ HERE IS WHERE EVIL REIGNS SUPREME

COULD THIS BE HELL.....
CUZ UGLINESS AND EVIL VISITS ME DAILY

COULD THIS BE HELL.....
CUZ DARKNESS RULES EVEN THE DAY

COULD THIS BE HELL.....
CUZ SOMETIMES IT'S HARD TO
IMAGINE ANYTHING WORSE

COULD THIS BE HELL....
CUZ IT SEEMS TO NEVER END

COULD THIS BE HELL.....
CUZ THE PAIN I'VE FELT SHOULD NOT BE SO

COULD THIS BE HELL.....
CUZ MANY OF US VIEW IT AS HAPPINESS

COULD THIS BE HELL.....
CUZ WE THINK WE ARE RIGHTEOUS

COULD THIS BE HELL.....
CUZ I FEEL TRAPPED AND I YEARN TO ESCAPE

COULD THIS BE HELL.....
CUZ I'M TRAPPED IN A BODY
THAT'S CONDEMNED TO DIE

COULD THIS BE HELL.....
CUZ AFTER SO MANY YEARS
MY SOUL HAS NO REST

COULD THIS BE HELL.....
CUZ NO ONE SEEMS WILLING
TO DIE FOR THE TRUTH

COULD THIS BE HELL..... CUZ THE
PRESENCE OF TRUTH FADES DAILY

COULD THIS BE HELL.....
CUZ HERE IS WHERE IT'S SO
DIFFICULT TO SERVE HIM

COULD THIS BE HELL.....CUZ WE KILLED GOD

A True Warrior

HE STEPS FORWARD SWORD FIRMLY IN HAND.
DARING ANY OPPOSITION TO
OPPOSE HIS STAND.

HEAD HIGH, EYES PIERCING, FEET
FIRMLY ON THE GROUND.
WHY TRY, ONE CAN'T DENY
A GREATER PASSION CAN'T BE FOUND.

YET THERE IS A CHALLENGER WHO
STEPS BOLDLY TO THE FRONT.
HE SPEAKS NOT A WORD BUT HIS
INTENTIONS ARE ALL TO BLUNT.

THIS IS NO STANDOFF THE TRUE
WARRIOR CHARGES AHEAD.
THE ESSENCE OF BRAVERY, BY THE
LIGHT OF TRUTH HE'S LED.

POWERFUL BEINGS ARE NOW
LOCKED IN A STRUGGLE OF WILL.
ONE FAITH TO BE REVEALED THE
OTHER BOUND TO KNEEL.

THE TRUE WARRIOR'S STRENGTH RISES
AS THE CHALLENGER'S QUICKLY FADES.
WHAT SEEMED AN IMPOSSIBLE CONQUEST
NOW FALLS VICTIM TO TRUTH'S BLADE.

TRUTH HAS PREVAILED AND
NO FOE CAN STAND.
THE TRUE WARRIOR LOOKS TOWARD THE SKY
AND RAISES HIS MIGHTY HAND.

A WAR CRY OF DEVOTION IS TRIUMPHANTLY
RELEASED FROM HIS LIPS.
ANOTHER VICTORY FOR THE TRUTH,
FROM THE WELL OF GOD HE SIPS.

EVERLASTING LIFE, A WORLD WITHOUT
END THE TRUE WARRIOR HAS WON ALL.
STILL, HE MOVES ON TO FACE ANOTHER FOE
AND TRUTH ALONE STANDS TALL.

THE PERSONIFICATION OF LIFE,
LED BY AN ETERNAL LIGHT,
THE ESSENCE OF POWER FROM ON HIGH.
YOU SEE IT IS BECAUSE OF THIS
A TRUE WARRIOR FIGHTS,
REALIZING THAT ANY DAY IS
A GOOD DAY TO DIE.

Death Is Imminent

DEATH IS IMMINENT, ETERNAL
LIFE HAS NO PART IN SELF.
DEATH IS IMMINENT, FIGHTING
IT SHALL NOT PREVAIL.
DEATH IS IMMINENT, YET WE FOLLY WITH IT.
DEATH IS IMMINENT, INDEED TRUE
BEAUTY LIES WITHIN IT.

DEATH IS IMMINENT,
YET UNDERSTANDING IT REMAINS A MYSTERY.

DEATH IS IMMINENT, AND
THAT MAKES ME HAPPY.
DEATH IS IMMINENT, IN FACT IT IS
GREATER THAN THIS LIFE.
DEATH IS IMMINENT, HOW
THEN SHALL WE LIVE?
DEATH IS IMMINENT, YET
TEARS ALWAYS FLOW.
DEATH IS IMMINENT, WE DIE ALONE.
DEATH IS IMMINENT, IT IS OUR ONLY ESCAPE.
DEATH IS IMMINENT, YET WHO
AMONG US EMBRACES IT.

DEATH IS IMMINENT,
WHO AMONG US CAN ESCAPE
THIS FREEDOM?

DEATH IS IMMINENT, YET IT
NEVER TRULY EXISTED.
DEATH IS IMMINENT, IT IS THEN
WE WILL AWAKEN.
DEATH IS IMMINENT, IT IS THEN
OUR JOURNEY TRULY BEGINS

Unconditional Luv

UNCONDITIONAL LUV
HOW UNFORTUNATE IT IS THAT
WE LACK THE CAPACITY TO GIVE
THE GREATEST GIFT OF ALL.

UNCONDITIONAL LUV
HOW STRANGE THAT WE DESIRE WHAT
NO HUMAN BEING CAN GIVE

UNCONDITIONAL LUV
HOW CARELESSLY WE USE THE
TERM YET NEVER POSSESSING THE
KNOWLEDGE TO UNDERSTAND IT.

UNCONDITIONAL LUV
WE SPEAK OF IT AS IF IT IS A REALITY
IN OUR WORLD, YET OUR WORLD
IS CORRUPT AND DYING.

UNCONDITIONAL LUV
HOW CAN SOMETHING THAT
REQUIRES A COMPLETE DEATH BE
EXPERIENCED BY THOSE ALIVE?

UNCONDITIONAL LUV
OUR WORLD OUR EXISTENCE
IS CONDITION AL;
WITHOUT THE OCCURRENCES OF
CERTAIN THINGS HOW WOULD WE

UNCONDITIONAL LUV
THE CONCEPT, THIS REALITY, THIS TRUTH
DOES NOT EXIST IN OUR WORLD

UNCONDITIONAL LUV
IN FACT, THE ONLY WAY WE CAN OR
EVER WILL EXPERIENCE IT..,
IS TO ESCAPE THIS WORLD THROUGH
THE PORTAL OF DEATH.

UNCONDITIONAL LUV

The Final Frontier

WHY I'M I LOST WITHIN MYSELF?
HOW CAN ONE BE FOUND IN
AN IMPERFECT STATE?

DO I DESIRE TO BE FOUND
AND IS IT TRULY ME?
YOU SEE IT IS ME THAT I'M SPEAKING TO.

WILL THIS SEARCH EVER BE COMPLETE?
ISN'T EVERYONE SEARCHING,
WHETHER THEY KNOW IT OR NOT?

ISN'T EVERYONE LOST, AREN'T WE ALL ALIKE?
DON'T WE ALL HAVE THE SAME QUESTION?

WE ARE INCOMPLETE, WE ARE
SO SMALL, SO POWERLESS.
WHAT OF US OR AMONGST US CAN
WE POSSIBLY TAKE OWNERSHIP?

WE CHERISH THAT WHICH IS
FADING AND INCONSISTENT.
WE ARE FAITHLESS, WE ARE
WITHOUT TRUE BELIEF.

DEATH IS NOT AN ENDING BUT A BEGINNING.
WE DON'T BELONG HERE, WE
ARE NOT TEMPORAL.

YOU DON'T UNDERSTAND ME.
I DON'T UNDERSTAND MYSELF.

WE LIVE IN THE UNKNOWN,
THE DARKNESS OF LIFE.
THERE IS NO SUCH THING AS AN
UNDERSTANDING, ONLY A SURRENDERING

WE HAVE LIFE ONLY WITHIN OURSELVES.
YET IT IS NOT US BUT RATHER THE UNKNOWN.

WE SEARCH FOR ANSWERS EVERYWHERE
AROUND US NEVER REALIZING.
YOU AND I ARE THE FINAL FRONTIER

The Connection

BLACK IS THE NIGHT YET
LOVELY IS ITS SOLITUDE.
YOU LOOK UP AT THE STARRY SKY
AND SEE THE WONDER OF WHO YOU ARE.

YOU ARE SO TRIVIAL YET YOU ARE
THE CENTER OF THE UNIVERSE.
FOR UNIVERSE IS WITHIN YOU
SO THERE IS NO ESCAPE.

SO SMALL IN THE MEASURE OF IT ALL.
YET EVEN YOU CAN MOVE
THE FORCES THAT BE.

HMM, THE FORCES THAT BE ONE
SIMPLY CANNOT DENY.
FOR WHAT'S GREATER THAN
YOU IS INSIDE OF YOU.

THE QUESTION IS WILL YOU EVER HEAR
HIM, TOUCH HIM, TRULY EXPERIENCE HIM.
YOU ASK THE QUESTION AND DEEP
DOWN KNOW THE ANSWER.

HOW CAN YOU DENY WHO YOU ARE.
THE COMPLEXITY OF YOURSELF
IS THE REALITY OF HIM.

YOU ARE NOT PHYSICAL, YOU
ARE NOT CONFINED,
YOU ARE NOT BOUND.
YOU ARE INTELLECT, YOU ARE THE WIND,
YOU ARE UNABATED.

YOU ARE INDEED BEYOND
THE WISDOM OF MAN.
YOU ARE A WONDER, YOU ARE A MYSTERY,
YOU ARE A QUEST.

WILL OUR SEARCH EVER END? INDEED IT
CANNOT IF WE WANT TO LIVE FOREVER.
YET THE REALITY IS KNOWING
WHERE YOUR SEARCH ENDS.

WHERE DOES YOUR SEARCH BEGIN?
THE DARKNESS OF THE NIGHT
HOLDS THE LIGHT OF REALITY.
IN THE DEEPEST RESOURCES OF YOUR
MIND AND SOUL LIES THE ANSWER.

HEAR HIM? "YES, IT IS I, I AM
WHOM YOU SEEK."
"WILL YOU ACKNOWLEDGE ME,
WILL YOU CHERISH ME,
WILL YOU COME TO ME?"

Knowledge of God

YOU MUST DIE, AND IT IS JUST THAT SIMPLE.
YET WE LIVE OUR LIVES
CONSTANTLY FIGHTING THIS.
THIS IS THE COURSE TRAVELED
FOR KNOWLEDGE OF GOD.
IT IS THE ONLY MEANS BY WHICH TO LEARN.

FOR WE WERE BORN IN THIS
STATE OF SEPARATION.
BUT GOD HAS PROVIDED A
MEANS FOR CONNECTION.
IN HIS INFINITE WISDOM, HE'S
SET OUR COURSE.
NOW WE MUST WALK IT,
FOR THIS IS THE KNOWLEDGE OF GOD.

OUR LIVES EXIST IN HIS WISDOM
FROM WHICH IS NO ESCAPE.
DO WE TRULY REALIZE WE
ARE NOT IN CONTROL?
HE WATCHES OUR BEGINNING AND
OUR ENDING ALL AT ONCE.

HOW SMALL YET SO RELEVANT
IS THE REALITY WE LIVE IN.

ETERNITY IS WITHIN HIM AND
TIME IS BUT A THOUGHT.
THIS IS THE KNOWLEDGE OF GOD
YET IT'S FOREIGN TO US.
HE'S IN ANOTHER DIMENSION
AND HE ALWAYS WILL BE.
IT'S JUST HIM BEING GOD
AND THIS IS GODLY KNOWLEDGE.

HOW CAN WE KNOW SUCH A GOD?
YET, HOW CAN WE NOT.
REALIZING WHO WE ARE
REVEALS WHO HE IS.
CAN WE TRULY EXPERIENCE
THE DEPTHS OF GOD?
HOW CAN WE WHEN WE DON'T DESIRE HIM.
THE KNOWLEDGE OF GOD
BEGINS WITHIN US.
KNOWING NOTHING IS WITHHELD
PRIORITIZES OUR DESIRE.

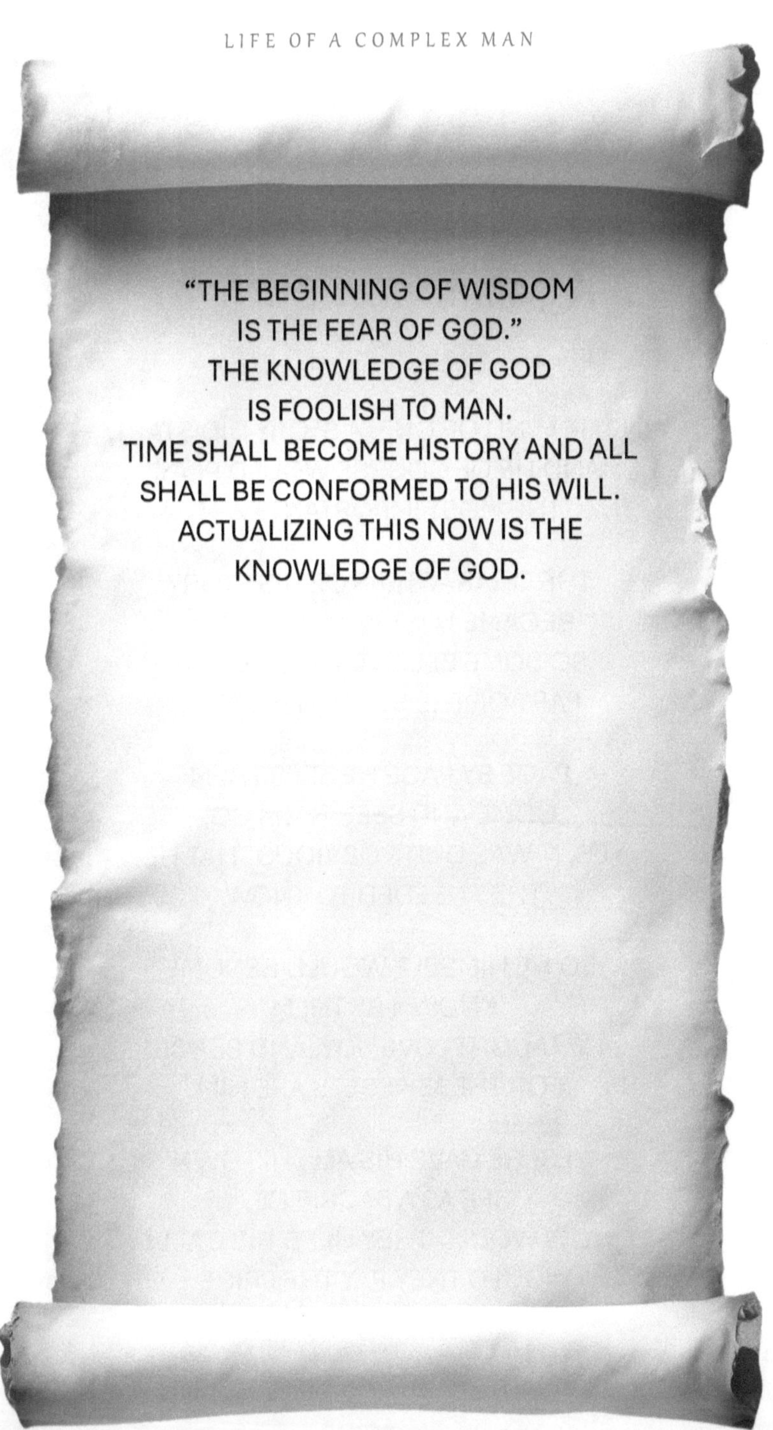

"THE BEGINNING OF WISDOM
IS THE FEAR OF GOD."
THE KNOWLEDGE OF GOD
IS FOOLISH TO MAN.
TIME SHALL BECOME HISTORY AND ALL
SHALL BE CONFORMED TO HIS WILL.
ACTUALIZING THIS NOW IS THE
KNOWLEDGE OF GOD.

Redemption's Story

IN THE MIND OF ONE, A STORY DID START,
AND HE OF COURSE WOULD PLAY
THE MOST IMPORTANT PART

THE CHARACTERS OF HIS STORY
BECAME LOST WITH NO HOPE
SO SOME BELIEVE THEY'RE NOT
PART OF THE STORY HE WROTE

PAGE BY PAGE HE SEES THEM
COME AND SEES THEM GO,
YES, IT WAS QUITE OBVIOUS THAT HE,
THEY NEEDED TO KNOW.

SO HE HIMSELF WOULD BECOME
KNOWN BY THEM.
HE TAUGHT LOVE, JOY, AND PEACE
FOR THESE ASSETS ARE HIM

YES, HE GAVE HIS ALL, HIS OWN
LIFE AS A SACRIFICE,
NOW WOULD THEY HEED HIS CALL,
WOULD THEY PAY THE PRICE.

WOULD HE BE RECOGNIZED AS THE
GREAT AUTHOR OF THIS STORY,
OR WOULD THEY TRY TO CREATE THEIR
DESTINIES FOR THEIR GLORY.

THIS STORY MUST END JUST
AS ALL STORIES DO,
AND IT'S TO US IN PARTICULAR
IT'S RELEVANT TO.

SO DO YOU RECOGNIZE THIS STORY
CAUSE IT RELATES TO YOUR SOUL,
OR HAS YOUR MIND GONE REPROBATE
AS TIME HAS TAKEN ITS TOLL.

WHO IS THIS AUTHOR, YOU
ASK IN YOUR MIND.
YET FAITH IS WHAT IT TAKES TO FIND.

FOR IT'S FAITH IN HIM THAT YOU
WILL FIND NO EXEMPTION.
JESUS IS HIS NAME AND HIS STORY
IS CALLED REDEMPTION.

What Luv Is

YOU DON'T KNOW WHAT **LUV IS**.............
HOW CAN YOU WALK AWAY FROM IT

YOU DON'T KNOW WHAT **LUV IS**............
GIVE LUV A CHANCE.

YOU DON'T KNOW WHAT **LUV IS**............
YET I REFUSE TO LEAVE YOU.

YOU DON'T KNOW WHAT **LUV IS**............
AND YOU SUFFER BECUZ OF IT.

YOU DON'T KNOW WHAT **LUV IS**............
BECUZ YOU'RE SCARED TO FACE IT.

YOU DON'T KNOW WHAT **LUV IS**............
IT RESIDES BEYOND THE FLESH.

YOU DON'T KNOW WHAT **LUV IS**............
WHY LIVE AS IF YOU DO.

YOU DON'T KNOW WHAT **LUV IS**............
LUV IS WITHOUT QUESTION...
WITHOUT THOUGHT.

YOU DON'T KNOW WHAT **LUV IS**.............
LUV IS NOT FOUND.

YOU DON'T KNOW WHAT **LUV IS**............
BECUZ LUV NEVER FAILS.

YOU DON'T KNOW WHAT **LUV IS**............
LUV IS IN PAIN.

YOU DON'T KNOW WHAT **LUV IS**............
LUV IS DEAD.

YOU DON'T KNOW WHAT **LUV IS**............
LUV NEVER DIES.

YOU DON'T KNOW WHAT **LUV IS**............
LUV IS NOT EXPERIENCED.

YOU DON'T KNOW WHAT **LUV IS**............
LUV SIMPLY IS.

Laying It Down

YOU'VE GOT TO DIE, YOU'VE GOT TO
STOP LIVING FOR YOURSELF.
WHY, CAUSE IT'S IN DYING
THAT WE FIND OURSELF.

IT'S IN DYING THAT WE COME TO
OUR MEANING, OUR PURPOSE,
IT'S IN DYING WE FIND AMBITIONS
BECOME TRULY WORTHLESS.

WE'VE COME TO THE REALITY
THAT WE MUST SELL OUT.
NO QUESTIONS ALLOWED
THERE'S SIMPLY NO DOUBT.

FOR WE MUST BE DISPLAYED AS
THE SALT OF THE EARTH.
A WORKMAN NOT ASHAMED
CREATING NEW BIRTH.

WE ARE LIVING FOR ANOTHER BECAUSE
ANOTHER PAID THE PRICE.
BEYOND THE LOVE OF ANY MOTHER
IT'S THE ULTIMATE SACRIFICE.

A HUMBLE SERVANT, PURE IN
NATURE, HOLY ONE WITH NO SIN.
INDEED NO GREATER SHOW OF
LOVE THERE EVER HAS BEEN.

HE WHO CAME SAW AND CONQUERED,
LOVE WRAPPED IN FLESH.
NAME ABOVE ALL NAMES, HIS
HOLY NAME I BLESS.

HE LAID IT DOWN, THAT'S WHAT
HE DID, A LIFE WITHOUT,
AND BEYOND UNDERSTANDING.
MY LIFE IN HIM NOW FULLY HIS,
TOTALLY COMMITTED TO HIS
EVERY COMMAND.

HE LAID IT DOWN, THEN PICKED IT UP,
HIS LIFE IS NOW CALLED EVERLASTING.
I CAN'T BE FOUND, CAUSE I'M CAUGHT UP,
IN FOLLOWING HIM AND NEVER PASSING.

YES, I'M AMAZED, I'M OVERJOYED,
IT'S ALL BECAUSE REAL LOVE I'VE FOUN D.
JESUS, YOU'RE MY ALL IN
ALL, GOD ALMIGHTY,
FOR YOU TRULY LAID IT DOWN.

The Lost and Found

MONEY, SEX, AND POWER...THE VICES
WHICH CONTROL OUR SOCIETY
IF WE COULD LIVE WITHOUT THE NEED
OF THESE WHAT KIND OF
WORLD WOULD WE BE?
RELIGION, WAR, TRADITION....
THE UNAVOIDABLES OF LIFE
WITHIN OUR WORLD.

IS IT POSSIBLE TO LIVE ABOVE
THESE INEVITABLES, TO FUNCTION
IN COMPLETE PEACE?
YES, I BELIEVE IT IS.....
THE QUESTION IS HOW MANY
PEOPLE WANT THIS?

I HAVE FOUND PEOPLE'S WORDS ARE
FAR REMOVED FROM THEIR ACTIONS.
INDEED, IT IS HOW WE TREAT ONE
ANOTHER THAT IS SO SINFUL.
STILL YET, SOME OF US TREAT OURSELVES
WITH GROSS UNRIGHTEOUSNESS.

WE ALL KNOW AND HAVE THE
ABILITY TO LOVE, TO GIVE,
TO BECOME COMPLETELY SELFLESS .
WE ARE AFRAID, WE'RE CARELESS,
WE'RE IGNORANT, WE ARE LOST.
SOMEDAY WE WILL BE FOUND
AND THAT CHOICE, THAT DAY,
WILL BE COMPLETELY OURS.

My Word Play

EVERYONE PLAYS WITH WORDS IN
SOME FORM OR ANOTHER,
SO ALLOW ME TO BE HEARD. CHECK
OUT MY PLAY OF WORDS.....
MY WORDPLAY.

PERMIT MY FOLLY....MY FOLLY
PERMIT, LEST, BEFORE THE END OF
MY POEM, YOU BEG ME TO QUIT.
IF I WAS THE VOICE OF GOD.....
WOULD YOU LISTEN?
I HAVE SOMETHING TO SAY, SOMETHING THAT
JUST MIGHT BRIGHTEN YOUR DAY, IF I MAY.
YOU'VE BEEN CHOSEN TO BE HONORED....
PRIVILEGED TO BE CHOSEN.
HONORED TO BE PRIVILEGED TO
EXPERIENCE THE JOY OF MY WORDPLAY...

...TODAY, I PLAY AND WITH PLEASURE, I MAY.
MAY I, STIMULATE YOUR MIND.....IN HOPES
THAT YOU'LL FIND. SOME THINGS ARE MEANT
TO HAPPEN IN TIME....JUST AS YOU HAVE
STUMBLED UPON MY RHYME.

YET I PROMISE TO EDUCATE, THE SIMPLEST
OF TRUTHS I'LL RELATE.....MAYBE TO SUCH
THAT YOU HAVE NOT HEARD....BUT REALIZE
IT'S SIMPLY MY PLAY OF WORDS.
MAY I STIMULATE YOUR MIND....WITH
THESE FEW MEASURES OF RHYME.
YET RHYMING IS NOT THE KEY.....
AND BEFORE WE'RE DONE
PROMISE THIS YOU WILL SEE.
WHAT IS THE DEFINITION OF HEAVEN?
COULD IT BE, SHOULD IT BE A PLACE
OR SIMPLY A STATE OF BEING
WOULD IT BE, COULD IT BE FAIR
TO SAY IT'S A PLACE OR A STATE OF
ETERNAL PEACE AND HAPPINESS.
MAYBE, IT COULD BE, THAT WE, DO
NOT SEE, THINGS SO DIFFERENTLY
COULD IT BE, I'VE FOUND SOME
COMMON GROUND, BETWEEN YOU
AND ME? INDEED NO LONGER BOUND,
BY THIS IGNORANCE AROUND
BOTH YOU ARE ME.

ALLOW MY WORDS TO PLAY, PLAY WITH
MY WORDS...YOU MAY SE THINGS MUCH
LIKE ME, AFTER THE HARMONY OF
THOUGHTS....BETWEEN YOU AND ME.

ALLOW ME TO COMMUNICATE,
I AND YOUR STATE,
JUST HOW WE RELATE.
COME WITH ME ON A JOURNEY
INTO THE DARK......
IN HOPES I'LL SPARK, THAT FLAME,
JUST THE SAME, AND MAYBE
YOU'LL REMEMBER MY NAME.

GIVE ME JUST A SECOND, AND I RECKON,
WE MIGHT GET TO REFLECTION.....ON
THIS DAY, THIS TIME, THIS MOMENT,
THIS VERY NOW YOU MIGHT WONDER
HOW.....DID I CAPTIVATE YOUR MIND,
WITH THIS RHYTHM, THIS RHYME....YET
IT'S MY PLAY, MY PLAY OF WORDS.....
YA HEARD, MY WORDS, MY PLAY. TODAY I MAY,
MAY I TODAY, STIMULATE YOUR MIND, AND
IN TIME YOU'LL FIND, IT'S QUITE NICE TO
WITNESS THE GROOVE OF THIS RHYME.
IF I TOLD YA ME, AND YOU WERE
DESTINED TO BE.....
WOULD YOU BELIEVE ME? YET,
WHAT I SPEAK IS REALITY, BECAUSE
ME, AND YOU ARE HERE NOW.

EXPERIENCING NOW, RELATING
NOW, SHARING NOW,
COMMUNICATING NOW, DESTINED
NOW. THE HOW, AND WHY WOULD
THIS, COULD THIS, SHOULD THIS BE
SO DIFFICULT TO UNDERSTAND.
ME AND YOU.......SYMBOLICALLY
HAND AND HAND, WE UNDERSTAND.
THESE WORDS, THIS NOW, THIS
DESTINY....BETWEEN YOU AND ME.
HMMM, THIS IS CRAZY YOU SAY....
BUT DEEP DOWN YOU DISPLAY,
THAT CONNECTION I FEEL, WHICH
IS REAL.....THIS DAY, THIS WAY.

SO THEN YOU'VE FALLEN, INTO THIS
THANG I'M MACK MAULING, NEVER
QUITE KNEW I WAS CALLING....
...ALL ALONG, SO STRONG MEANING
IT CAN'T BE AVOIDED.
YET AT THE END OF THIS JOURNEY,
YOUR PATIENCE AND ATTENTIVENESS
WILL BE DULY AWARDED.
JUST AS ANY TEST ENDS WITH A PRIZE,
YOU'LL FIND WHERE REST AND
PEACE OF MIND TRULY LIES.

AND HOW AMAZING IT IS THAT
YOU'LL FIND IT TODAY
AMID MY FOLLY MY SIMPLE WORDPLAY.

WORDS EXPRESS MEANING,
MEANING SO VAST,
AND INDEED IT IS OUR WORDS THAT
ULTIMATELY LIVE ON AND LAST AND
WE'VE TAKING IT LIGHTLY HOW
WE'VE EXPRESS OUR WORDS
MANY TIMES NOT CARING EXACTLY
HOW THEY MAY HAVE BEEN HEARD.

SO BE CAREFUL MY FRIEND AND
TAKE THIS THOUGHT WITH YOU TIL THE END.

IT'S A JOY TO EXPERIENCE LIFE BUT WHAT JOY
IS THERE UNLESS YOU GIVE COMPLETELY
OF YOURSELF TO ONE WHO ACCEPTS YOU,
LOVES YOU UNCONDITIONALLY.

YOU SEE, NO LOVE IS NO LIFE,
NO LIFE IS WHERE WE
SOMETIMES THINK WE ARE.

BUT MY FRIEND I LOVE YOU, THINK NOT THAT
THE AUTHOR OF THIS POEM IS SPEAKING.
YET REALIZE IT'S THE VOICE FROM WITHIN
YOURSELF, CALLING, SPEAKING,
PULLING, TUGGIN AT YOUR HEART
JUST NOW THIS MOMENT THIS DAY.

YET YOU'VE EXPERIENCED THIS REALITY,
THIS REALNESS WITHIN THIS SIMPLE
VET COMPLEX POEM TODAY,
MY WAY, IF I MAY CONVEY,
AND ALLOW ME TO RELAY,
EVEN SAY AND PORTRAY....
WITHIN THE CONFINES OF MY WORDPLAY.

* 9 7 8 1 9 6 9 9 1 9 5 9 6 *